I started hunting when I was only eleven! But I don't mean hunting on horseback.

When I go hunting, I lie in wait for some animal or bird, and then I shoot it – with my camera!

There aren't many boys of my age out in the country where I live, so photography is a good hobby for me.

One Friday, my father, who is a vet, came home looking rather worried.

"Mr. Fielding lost some chickens last night," he told me. "A fox got into his runs. But I can't understand why a fox should go after chickens in the spring."

"Someone shot a fox in Coker Copse last week," I said. "Perhaps this one is his mate, and has cubs to feed."

"Perhaps," my father replied. "If so, then her home could be somewhere around there."

"Well, I know where I'm going tomorrow, then," I told him.

"Up to the copse. I might get a photograph of the cubs."

My father smiled and said, "You just try finding them!"

Saturday was fine and sunny;
almost perfect for photography.
I set off early for Coker Copse
with my camera, a spare film,
and some sandwiches.

I wandered about most of
the morning, and found a lot
of rabbit holes, but nothing
that looked like a fox's earth.

Then I came to a clearing.

A shallow stream ran along
one end, and at the other
a pile of logs lay rotting.

In the middle, one big oak
tree had been left standing.
Its roots dug into the ground
like huge fingers.

About half way up,
I could see a kind of
double fork in the branches.

Just the place to build
a tree house, I thought.
I was fed up with looking
for foxes, anyway.

Down by the pile of logs
were some dead branches
that had been lopped off.
I found a length of old rope
lying there, too.

I climbed up the tree
with the rope, and then
ran it over a projecting
branch, like a crane.

After that, it was easy
to pull some dead branches
up. Soon I had a floor
that would take my weight.

I made the walls
of thinner branches,
and finished them off
with bits of bracken.

It had been hard work,
and I decided to sit up
in the tree house
and eat my sandwiches.

I took my camera up
with me as well.

Through the hole in
the floor, I had a good view
right across the clearing.

After a while, a couple
of young rabbits appeared,
and started to play in
the sunshine.

They were too far away
to photograph, so I just
watched them.

Suddenly one sat upright,
and his nose started twitching.
Then he thumped the ground
with his back legs.

That means he's going
to run, I thought. But why?

Both rabbits slipped away
into the bushes, and everything
went very quiet.

A minute or two passed.
I kept looking round,
but there was nothing in sight.

Then I froze. The bracken
on the far side moved slightly,
and a beautiful brown vixen
slid into view.

She stood perfectly still,
sniffing this way and that,
until she was sure it was safe.
Then she moved across
to the stream, splashed up it
for a few yards, and came out
on my side of the clearing.

Why was she trying to
kill her scent, I wondered.

Now the vixen was making
for my tree! I picked up
my camera excitedly.
But there was something funny
about the way she moved,
sniffing and listening
all the time.

Then there was a rustle
at the foot of the tree.
I looked down and very nearly
dropped my camera.

One . . . two . . . three . . .
little heads were poking out
from behind a root.

Cubs!

I could hardly believe my eyes.
I must have made my tree house
right above the vixen's earth.

So that is why she had been
so careful about her scent,
I thought. With any luck
I could get a shot of vixen
and cubs playing together.

A fourth cub struggled out.
He was even smaller than
the others. They began to
tumble about, while the vixen
licked them.

Click! went my camera,
and the vixen looked up,
ears pricked and nose twitching.

She was staring straight at me
but her eyes were dull
and half-shut.

She was nearly blind!

Some way off, a twig cracked
sharply. A dog barked, and
I heard a man's voice.

Someone was coming.

Already the half-blind vixen
was pushing her cubs back
to the safety of the earth.

She picked the last one up
in her mouth, and dropped it
out of sight.

But it wasn't the last;
the smallest cub was running
unsteadily across the clearing
to the pile of logs.
Then he disappeared
right underneath them.

The vixen sniffed round
the tree, but the cub was gone.

As the barking grew louder,
the vixen ran back through
the stream and melted
into the bracken again.

I didn't want anyone to find
my new tree house, so I climbed
down as quickly as I could.

Now I could see
the fox's earth, hidden under
one of the thicker roots.

As my feet touched the ground,
a small fox terrier burst
through the bracken.

"Find him, Whisky," said
a voice, and Mr. Fielding
walked up the path
into the clearing.

He was carrying a shot gun,
and he had two bigger dogs
with him.

"Hello, Mr. Fielding,"
I said. "Shooting rabbits?"

"Not really," he answered.

"I'm after the vixen that's been killing my chickens. It's been seen out this way."

The young terrier had gone down to the stream for a drink. Now he was coming back towards us, sniffing at the ground, and yelping excitedly.

He must have picked up the vixen's scent!

"He's after something," said the farmer, cocking his shotgun.

Suddenly the terrier ran between my legs and disappeared. He had found the hidden entrance to the vixen's earth.

The other dogs crouched
by the hole, waiting.

Mr. Fielding bent over
the hole. "That's a fox's
earth all right," he said.
"And something's down there,
too. Good dog, Whisky.
Fetch it out then, boy!"

Snarling, whining noises
came from deep in the hole.

"What happens if young cubs
are down there?" I asked,
with my heart thumping.

The farmer frowned.

"Whisky's got to learn
how to hunt," he said.
"It'll do him good to taste
blood. Cubs or foxes,
it's all the same to me.
They're no use to farmers."

Something was coming
out of the earth.
The farmer raised his gun,
but it was only the terrier,
wagging his tail.

"Go on, Whisky," said
Mr. Fielding, pushing
the terrier down the hole again.
"Chase 'em out, boy."
I turned and walked off.
I didn't want to see
what was bound to happen.
The thought of the cubs
being killed sickened me.

Then I noticed something
moving through the bracken
beyond the stream.

Now I could just make out
a pointed face and two
pricked up ears.

The vixen hadn't run away;
she was hiding there,
trying to see what was happening
to her cubs!

Behind me there was a shout
and a lot of yelping
as one of the cubs shot out of
another hole nearby, with
the terrier close behind.

The vixen bounded into
the open, leapt the stream,
and was across the clearing
like an arrow.

She blundered into the terrier
and snapped at his ear.
Then she ran past the farmer,
right across the clearing
and up the side of the track.
She was trying to draw
the dogs away from her cub.
What courage that poor
half-blind vixen has, I thought,
hoping she would get clear.

"Back, Whisky. Get back
will you!" cried the farmer,
raising his gun.

The vixen was almost
at the last corner of the track
when the farmer fired.

All three dogs raced forwards,
snarling and barking.

"I hit her," said the farmer.
"She won't get far now."

He ran after his dogs,
and I looked at the earth,
feeling miserable.

One cub had got clear,
but the dogs would soon
find the others when
they came back.

How I wished I could
get them out and save them.

Bang! went the farmer's gun
again. The vixen had given her
life trying to save her cubs,
but if the dogs came back again
her courage would have been
wasted.

Then suddenly I remembered
the smallest cub, hiding
in the pile of logs.

I ran over and poked about
in the wood, but I couldn't
see it anywhere.

Now I could hear the dogs

barking as they came back.
If I didn't find that cub,
they would. But where had
it gone?

One of the logs had
a hollow end. I reached up
inside and jumped as I felt
something warm and furry.

The cub!

Quickly I pulled him out,
pushed him down my windcheater
and ran.

Soon I was out of Coker Copse
and heading for home.

By the time I reached
our house, the cub wasn't
quite so frightened.

He was poking his head
out of my windcheater,
and sniffing at all
the strange smells around him.

Jenny, our golden spaniel,
came running out to meet me,
wagging her tail.
Then she saw the cub's head,
and began to whine softly.

She thought I had taken
one of her young puppies!

My father was standing
by the door, and he made
the same mistake.

"Give Jenny her pup back,"
he called. "You'll upset her."

I grinned and didn't say
a thing.

My father came closer.

"Don't tell me it's a cub,"
he said. "Now how on earth
did you get hold of that?"

I explained what had happened.

"I can't say I blame you,"
my father said. "But keep him
away from Jenny. Bring him
inside."

We took the cub into
the kitchen and shut the door.

"It's late for a vixen
to have cubs," my father told me.
"And this one's very young,
and a bit on the small side,
too. We'll have to feed him
on milk."

He fetched a toy feeding
bottle that he sometimes used
for feeding very young animals.

Then he filled it with
warm milk and tried to get
the cub to suck.

But it wouldn't.

"We've got to get some food
into him soon, or all your
trouble will have been
for nothing," my father said,
frowning thoughtfully.

"Yes," I agreed.
"And talking of trouble,
Trouble would be
a good name for him!"

"You're so right," sighed my
father, putting the bottle down.

Jenny was outside, scratching
and whining to be let in.

My father scratched his
chin thoughtfully. Then
he picked up Trouble.

"Let Jenny in," he said
to me. "Go on; open the door."

I turned the door handle
and Jenny padded in, whining.

"She still thinks Trouble
is one of her puppies," said
my father thoughtfully.

He held the cub out
and let Jenny sniff it. Suddenly
she stood up on her back legs
and took Trouble in her mouth!

I held my breath, but the cub
didn't seem frightened.

Did Jenny really think Trouble
was a puppy, or would she
smell he was a fox and kill him?
    Jenny trotted out of the
kitchen carrying the cub by
the scruff of his tiny neck.
We followed close behind.

She padded over to the
outhouse, where three puppies
lay in her basket. She climbed in
and dropped Trouble
gently alongside them.

She had adopted him!

"Well," said my father,
as we watched Trouble cuddle up
to his new mother. "He'll
be all right for food now."

Trouble was a wonderful pet.
Soon we were able to feed him
on bread and milk, and later
he ate Jenny's dog biscuits.
After he caught his first mouse,
he began to want
raw meat as well.

He was quite tame,
and I played with him
just as I did with Jenny's
own puppies.

He loved romping in the garden.
I made sure he couldn't get out,
in case any stray dogs
were about.

If it hadn't been for
his brush and pointed ears,
you couldn't really have told
him from a half-grown puppy.

The farmer's terrier was
inside the car, barking
and snarling, but it couldn't
get out. Trouble didn't
take any notice, because
he had never known a dog
who was an enemy.

When the farmer came back,
he couldn't believe his eyes.

A fox, calmly sitting in
the middle of the road,
eating one of his rabbits!

I heard him shouting
and ran out, but I was too late.
The farmer threw his stick
at Trouble, and flung open
the car door.

The dog flew at the fox,
and for the first time
Trouble knew fear. He dodged
the snapping jaws, dived
through the hedge and was
off across the fields.

"He may come back," my father
said, when he heard what had
happened. "We'll leave
the outhouse door open,
and put some meat there."

41

I didn't sleep well that night. I kept dreaming that Trouble was being hunted.

Once I woke up and heard a noise outside. I went to the window, and shone my torch down into the outhouse, but it was only Jenny getting comfortable in her basket.

In the morning Trouble was still missing.

"It looks as though he's gone for good," my father said, sadly. He had grown as fond of the young fox as I.

We left the outhouse door open for a week, but then we gave up.

Summer turned to autumn,
and I heard nothing more
of Trouble.

Coming home from school
one afternoon, I overheard
some men talking about hunting.

"Saturday, then," one was
saying. "It's a good enough
reason for starting early."

"Isn't it a bit soon for fox-hunting?" I asked my father when I reached home. "I heard some men talking and it sounded as though there was going to be a meet this Saturday."

My father looked unhappy.

"I didn't want to tell you," he said slowly. "The local farmers have asked the hunt to go out."

"But why?"

My father rubbed his chin.

"They're complaining about a young fox that's started raiding their chicken runs. It killed six last night."

"Not – not *Trouble*?"

Gazing out of the window my father said, "I'm not sure. But they say it's a young fox that isn't afraid to get into runs close to farm houses, even when dogs are about."

"They can't hunt a half-grown, half-tame fox," I protested.

"That's not the way the farmers look at it, and you can't really blame them," answered my father.

"If he's started killing chickens there's not much we can do. All the same, it's a bit unfair. Trouble doesn't know what hunting is all about. He doesn't

46

realise that a pack of hounds
will be out for his blood."
I felt miserable.
Trouble had been such a
beautiful, friendly cub.
I hated to think of him being
hunted to death.

Lying in bed on Friday
night, I made up my mind
that I would do what I could
to warn Trouble.
I had a plan.

The following morning
I got up very early
and hunted through my drawers.
   At last I found what I
was looking for: an old
cap gun that I used to play with.
Luckily some rolls of caps
were in the drawer, too.

After breakfast, I slipped
out of the house without
letting anyone know
where I was going.

I set off across the fields
towards the copse. That was
where Trouble was most likely
to be, I thought to myself.

When I got there,
I walked about, firing
my cap gun. It made a good
loud bang, and my plan was
to scare Trouble away, if he
was here, before the hunt started.

Soon I had used up
all the caps. I scared some
pigeons and a red squirrel,
but I didn't see any sign
of a fox.

My old tree house was
still there, but it was
looking a bit shaky, though.

I climbed up into it.

The leaves were falling, and
now I could see the open country
lying beyond the copse.

In the distance I could just
make out the hunt moving slowly
across the fields. Then they
moved more quickly, and faintly
I heard the sound of a horn.

They must have put up
a fox. Could it be Trouble,
as far away as that?

Then I remembered the hunt;
they might be coming through
the copse. I could hear faint
shouts, and dogs yapping in
the distance, but now the hunt
seemed to be going away again.

A single dog crossed
into the clearing and stopped.
I stared and stared.

It wasn't a dog at all.
It was Trouble the Fox!

His tongue was hanging out,
and his sides were heaving. He
seemed tired and frightened.

He looked round the clearing,
but he didn't see me lying there.
Then he ran to the stream,
splashed along it and climbed
back on the same side.

He was trying to confuse
the dogs by doubling back
on his tracks! But if he did,
I thought, trying not to move
despite the pain, the hunt might
not come as far as the clearing.

"Trouble!" I shouted weakly.

Trouble stopped; ears cocked
and one foot held in the air,
just like a big puppy. He half
wanted to come to me; but now
he was scared of human beings.

Then he crossed the stream
and padded slowly up
towards me, his fine brush
trailing behind him.

He still knew me!

I could hear hounds
making for the copse. They were
bound to find me if Trouble
stayed where he was. But was it
fair for him to save my life –
and then lose his own?

He stood near me, panting.
What a fine-looking fox he was
now, I thought. How could I
protect him from the hunt?

My fingers poked about
in the grass as I thought hard.
Then I felt a hollow. A hole –
it was Trouble's old home!

"Down here, Trouble," I called.
But Trouble didn't move.
I was a human being,
and he wasn't sure if he could
trust even me that close.

Suddenly hounds filled
the clearing and the first
huntsmen rode down the track.

Trouble's ears went back
and he trembled. Then he
shot down the earth to safety.

As the hounds raced across
the clearing, I gritted my teeth
and turned so that my legs
covered Trouble's hiding place.

Hounds bayed and barked
angrily all around me, and
I saw their sharp teeth and
snapping, dripping jaws.

So that's what it's like
to be hunted down, I thought.

"Whip them off; there's a boy
here who's hurt himself," a voice
shouted.

59

The hounds were called off,
and some huntsmen dismounted
and came over to me.

"I fell out of the tree,"
I said. "I think I've broken
my back. It hurts a lot."

"Let's have a look," said
one of them. "I'm a doctor."

He ran his hands over me
and gently turned me
on to my side.

Suddenly the pain stopped
and the red-coated doctor
burst out laughing!

"Your back's not broken,"
he said, "but no wonder
it was hurting. This was
sticking right into you,"
and he handed me my cap gun.

"Come on, up you get."
"I think I'll rest here
for a bit first," I replied,
sliding back across the earth.
"Right-oh," the doctor said.
"We've lost our fox this time,
but we'll get him next Saturday."

When the hunt had gone,
I stood up. The doctor was
right; there was nothing
the matter with my back at all!

"Trouble?" I called, softly,
but there was no sign of him,
so I started off home.

Staying with me had nearly
cost him his life, I thought.
At least I had saved him
this time, but what chance
would he have next Saturday?

When I told my father about
Trouble, he said, "Don't worry;
I'll get him before Saturday."

"You're not going to shoot
him?" I said blankly.

My father showed me a wire
cage with a trap door.

"I'll bait this, leave it up in the copse, and trap him," he told me. "I've telephoned Pinbridge Zoo, and they're willing to give him a home."

But at the end of the week, the trap was still empty. The hunt didn't find Trouble, either, thank goodness.

He just vanished, and no one has seen anything of him round here since then.

I suppose it's just as well, really. At least, that's what I tell myself.

I still have that photograph of Trouble and his family. Sometimes I look at it, and wonder if I'll ever see him again.

Somehow I think I will.

So when farmers find me in fields marked 'private', and ask if I'm looking for trouble –
they're generally right!